JUST COSMIC

HOW TO FOLLOW YOUR ASTROLOGICAL TRANSITS

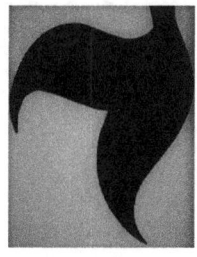

Rikki Blythe

Fishtail Arts & Astrology

www.fishtailastrology.com

THANK YOU: Steve McDowell – your excellent skill of placing and positioning concepts in time and space has made this manuscript far clearer. Elsa Moon - your time and dedication to the grammatical correctness of a bunch of words also greatly, beyond measure, improved the clarity of this manuscript. Thankfully Colin Ellis - the Untangler, also came in with a fine tooth comb. Without you three, I fear, the reader may have found these ideas difficult to understand. Many thanks also go to the Ladies of the Journal Trial Group; Bridget Carter, Evelyn Jill Allison, Georgia McRae, Heather Fraser, Kerry Anderson, Joanne Armstrong, Mandy Summers, Maz Pownall, Sharon Morgan, Mary Shewa, Sue Lancaster, Valeria Siretanu; you each brought great and valuable insights to the finished products. Thank you all.

Foreword

This book is nearly a complete copy of Cosmic Journal but without the pages for journaling. If you are going to create your own journal it is a very good idea to think about the layout. I recommend three pages for each Moon transit and a page each for the other transits. Put the Moon pages first as you will turn to them more often. If you journal with only linear dates you might not notice the patterns that happen at similar transits. Or you may already have your own ideas of how to record your transits, in which case you already know something about astrology. Perhaps Astro Journal – The Astrologer's Journal, which is already set out but has no instructions, would suit your needs. Either way, I hope you find a way to record your discoveries, so you can use your insights and be amazed at the subtleties of our natural connection with the cosmos.

CONTENTS

INTRODUCTION — - 5 -

KEY WORDS — - 8 -

WHERE TO START! — - 12 -

YOU WILL NEED — - 18 -

ILLUSTRATION *1 *2 *3 *4 — -19 - 22 -

UNDERSTANDING AN EPHEMERIS — - 23 -

EXTRAPOLATING CORRECT DATA — - 27-

CALCULATING TRANSITS — - 29 -

KNOWING WHAT TO LOOK FOR — - 38 -

KNOWING WHAT TO WRITE — - 41 -

PREPARING FOR TRANSITS — - 42 -

Introduction

For 30 years I have worked on astrology. I have met believers and I have met cynics; I said to them, "Prove it to yourself." The believers didn't need to and the cynics didn't know how. This is why I prepared Cosmic Journal and Just Cosmic; a guide for you to know when and where to look. If you wanted to see whether a bird existed, you would find out where to look. You would also find out what times that bird is likely to be in its habitat. Of course, you could hope to see this bird if it crossed your path but would you recognize it?

Objective proof provides rules so anyone can use the knowledge, to make bridges, fridges, gadgets and magnets for our wonderful modern world. Subjective proof is for one person; for example, psychology and counselling. The client is the only one who knows how the counselling helped. Psychology and counselling are similar to astrology in this respect. The astrologer – or anyone who can follow their transits - is the only one who can say, with certainty, "the Planets have an effect on me." Astrology can only be proved subjectively; you have to engage with it to know the truth. Cosmic Journal and Just Cosmic will bring to you the proof of the validity of astrology. These books are for beginners, believers and cynics alike. You will discover how to follow your transits.

> IF ASTROLOGY IS TRUE, IF THE PLANETS REALLY INFLUENCE US, THEN ACCEPTANCE OF THIS KNOWLEDGE WILL ALTER THE COURSE OF CIVILIZATION.

A long time ago I met a man who taught me astrology. I loved astrology. Astrology became my companion, my solace, my art and study. Then one day I thought I was mad to believe so much in astrology, so I spent two years trying to disprove it. During this time I kept strict journals of every Planet which transited my natal chart. I noted the conjunctions, squares, trines, oppositions and sextiles on every angle and every Planet in my horoscope. I watched other people's horoscopes too. Through my heartfelt attempt to disprove astrology I proved to myself that astrology works. The Planets have an influence on us that is expressed through our thoughts, ideas, inspirations, and moods.

Just Cosmic is a manual with explicit instructions on how to track the Sun, the Moon and astrological bodies as they transit your natal Sun, Moon, Planets, Nodes and Angles. Careful observation of the transits will reveal the influences which the astrological bodies have in your life. If you do not see any connection after watching your transits after 6 months or a year, you will still have been part of the research into the validity of astrology. You can contact Fishtail Arts & Astrology through the official website or Facebook page. There is a webpage dedicated to your findings and the findings of others.

Although I have found astrology to carry great validity, it is important to me that the truth is known worldwide. This is because the truth is so inspiring, so life transforming, it will alter masses of ideas between us and in ourselves. When we know that our behaviour and sense of self is influenced, despite incredible distances, our minds will broaden beyond imagination. The great truth of life will be laid bare in our times. We grow from inside till the day we die. The reality of our unity and our journey will be apparent. No longer will civilization be able to bury its head in the corrupted world of 'Me'.

Key Words

ANGLES The east horizon, west horizon and the highest and lowest point of the Sun's journey that day. These 4 points are extremely sensitive and can only be calculated from knowing the exact time of birth. They are shown as 4 points on the horoscope: Ascendant, Descendant, M.C and I.C respectively.

ASPECTS The relationship between Planets and Angles as a mathematical angle for example: 90° or 120°

ASTROLOGICAL BODIES Sun, Moon, Mercury, Venus, Mars, Jupiter, Saturn, Uranus, Neptune, Pluto, North Node, South Node, Ascendant, Descendant, M.C and I.C. All the Planets and points in space are put into the horoscope as significant because of their position in the Ecliptic Belt. The Sun, Moon and Planets were all grouped together as 'Planets' in ancient astrology.

CONJUNCT or CONJUNCTION 0° aspect between Planets in a natal chart as well as transiting Planets being in the exact place as a natal Planet.

CONSTELLATION **A constellation refers to a group of stars. In this book the constellations all refer to the zodiac constellations: Aries, Taurus, Gemini and so on.**

ECLIPTIC BELT **The Sun, all the Planets and Moon are all on the same plane in space. They appear to follow the same path around the earth. The path of the Sun, from rising, culmination to rising again is a ring around the earth. This ring, the Ecliptic Belt, is where the constellations of the zodiac are. The Sun, Moon and all the Planets cycle around in this ring.**

EPHEMERIS (Astrological) **Books of tables showing the Planets' and Nodes' daily positions within the Tropical Zodiac. This is a tiny pamphlet for a year, or it is a big book when it covers 50 years but it can also be found on-line. An astronomical ephemeris has different data to the astrological ephemeris.**

GMT **Greenwich Mean Time. All times will need converting to GMT to subsequently be converted to Sidereal Time; the time used in ephemerides (this is the plural of ephemeris).**

HOROSCOPE **Traditionally a horoscope is made up of 3 concentric circles in which the constellations and astrological bodies are placed.**

There are also square designs which are used in Jyotish astrology.

HOUSE A horoscope is divided into 12 segments in various ways. Placidus, Koch and Equal House are the main House systems. The Houses are called, 'first', 'second', 'third' and so on. Each House has a particular field of expression. The expression of 'nth' House is the same across each House system.

NODES In this book the Nodes always refer to the Moon's Nodes. These are points along the Ecliptic Belt on which the Sun and Moon's orbits intersect. They seemingly go backwards through the horoscope. These ancient points refer to karma (South Node) and future (North Node). They are significant to understanding some of your more deep seated tendencies which are difficult to get a handle on.

RETROGRADE As stated above, the Nodes go backwards; that is Retrograde. Planets also tend to appear to go backwards from our perspective on earth or they appear to stay still (though mostly they go forward – Direct). The larger Planets, due to their distance, appear Retrograde more often. This is significant when a transiting Planet is Retrograde on one of your natal Planets. In the ephemeris this is shown by R in the column of degrees of the relevant Planet. When the Planet turns direct, there is a D.

SIDEREAL TIME **The time used by astronomers to find the position of the Planets and stars in space. An ephemeris uses sidereal time from which the Angles of the Earth in relation to the stars can be calculated. Time of birth is converted to GMT and then is converted to sidereal time.**

TRANSIT **When a Planet or Node moves to the same position on your chart as one of your natal astrological bodies.**

UT **Universal Time is the same as GMT but all year round; it never changes to BST (British Summer Time).**

Where to Start!

Start by reading through all the instructions and familiarize yourself with this new subject. The instructions are concise and won't take long to read through. Even though the principles of astrology are quite simple, the order, of the simple building blocks, is different to what you have previously known. You are about to discover something very new.

For this project you can use either the Tropical Zodiac horoscope or the Sidereal Zodiac horoscope. The calculations of transits are the same for either zodiac. If you are using a Sidereal horoscope you will need to subtract 24° (Ayanamsa) from each Planet's position in the tropical based ephemeris. It is easy to tell if the ephemeris is based on the Tropical Zodiac by looking at the 21st or 22nd of a month. This is when the Sun would change signs. You are probably familiar with the Sun in Aries, 21st March till 20th April. Then Taurus follows in the following month, and so forth. This is the Tropical Zodiac. The Tropical Zodiac is prevalent in the West, as are ephemerides based on the Tropical Zodiac, so chances are you have a Tropical based horoscope and ephemeris. Please do not fixate on which zodiac to use - they both work - after this study you will understand why.

The Definitive Manual for the Calculations of Horoscopes and Transits[1] will guide you step-by-step to calculate your own horoscope and how to calculate transits too. Just Cosmic or Cosmic Journal will only guide you in calculating your transits.

It is a good idea to have your horoscope in front of you, so you can follow along as you read.

A horoscope is a snap-shot in time of the ecliptic belt with the constellations, Planets, Nodes and Angles.[2]

A horoscope is made up of 3 concentric rings. The outer ring shows the constellations. The middle ring shows the Planets, Nodes and House cusps, and subsequently shows which constellation they were in. Finally, the inner ring shows the Aspects that were formed between all the astrological bodies in that moment.

Your horoscope is like a snap-shot of the position of the Planets and constellations the moment you were born. It is like a London tube map in motion; the astrological bodies going around the centre (the birth of you on Earth) did not stop

---

[1] To be published 2019
[2] There are also asteroids, comets and Arabian Parts which can be added to the horoscope. You don't need all of these to prove astrology works, or even to reap an abundance of inner knowledge.

moving the moment you were born. Each Planet or Node has a cycle of its own.

The Moon travels around your horoscope once a month. The Sun, Mercury and Venus will travel a full cycle about once a year. Mars takes 2 years, Jupiter takes 12, Saturn takes 29, Uranus takes 84. Neptune and Pluto take much longer than our normal life time. The Nodes take 18 years.

When the transiting Sun conjuncts your Natal Sun, this is your birthday. Happy Birthday! Many happy returns is the ancient greeting which specifically means, many happy Solar returns – may the Sun return to the place in the sky that you were born, year after year.

Transits are when the Sun, Moon, Planets or Nodes travel to the same place in the sky as one of your natal Planets (in your horoscope). To track the transits, it is a good idea to start by working out the conjunctions. You can soon work out the other aspects.

A conjunction is an aspect. Aspects are the angles made between the astrological bodies in a natal horoscope, between horoscopes or between the heavens and your natal horoscope.

For example, aspects for the transiting Sun to your natal Sun would be: 6 months after your birthday, the transiting Sun is opposite your

Natal Sun and is called an OPPOSITION (180°). 3 months before and 3 months after your birthday, the transiting Sun SQUARES (90°) your Natal Sun. 4 months before and 4 months after your birthday, the transiting Sun TRINES (120°) your Natal Sun. Only on the day when the transiting Sun is at the same place as your Natal Sun, your birthday, is it CONJUNCT (0°). [3]

For learning to follow your transits (delineation) it is a good idea to begin with conjunctions so that you can begin today. A full explanation of how to calculate transits is given in the next chapter. It will not take long to pick up how to calculate the other aspects.

The Moon goes around the horoscope once a month. During the course of the next few years, you might not even watch an outer Planet's transit if you only consider conjunctions. You may choose to use other aspects for the outer Planets if no conjunctions occur over the next few years. Yet, the faster moving Planets will definitely make conjunctions. Sometimes a conjunction can happen over a few days or it comes back on itself in Retrograde and then turns Direct again. Later on you might want to

---

[3] The actual conjunction of Transiting Sun on Natal Sun can be as much as 8 hours' different from a birth time. Each year is slightly different, as the Sidereal day is not 24 hours, but 23 hours and 56 minutes.

add oppositions, squares and trines to your project.

When a transit occurs you need to record the results. By recording the results you will learn the influence of the Planets in your life and the profound significance of your birth horoscope. You might only need to write a few lines for a transit. Soon you will learn what you will look for when a transit happens.

Within a year you may notice the difference when Moon conjuncts a Planet and the other Planets form harmonious or inharmonious aspects with your Natal Moon. All of this can only be known by experience and over time you will get to know the 'feel' of the different astrological bodies within you. Do not be disappointed if after a few months you do not have amazing realizations, undoubtedly it will happen soon enough. It takes time and dedication to see the influences. Within a few months you will have had some realizations regarding the Moon, which will keep your inner-eye cocked for further incidents.

The outer Planets: Neptune and Pluto, may never conjunct one of your other Planets because their cycle is way beyond a normal life-span. Uranus is also one of the outer Planets but it will conjunct all of the astrological bodies in your natal horoscope if you have a long life.

Neptune and Pluto will, throughout an average lifetime, form some aspects but that is dependent on where they are in your horoscope. Many people who are interested in mystical and new-age traditions tend to have strong outer Planet transits; they are naturally drawn to understanding a sense of transformation which comes over them. If you do not have them, it may be because your sense of transformation is naturally more fluid. Outer Planet transits conjuncting personal Planets are rare and very powerful.

It is definitely still possible to prove the validity of astrology to yourself, just by watching the personal Planets. The personal Planets are: Sun, Moon, Mercury, Venus, Mars, Jupiter and Saturn. The personal Planets affect parts of your psyche which everyone uses day to day. To understand the outer Planets you will need to look outside the box and consider a wider scope of awareness.

You Will Need

Firstly you need a list of symbols. Lists of symbols are on the following pages. (Illustration *1,*2 and *3) These make up the language of astrology. The more you familiarize yourself with the symbols the easier it will be. It will help if you copy out the symbols in order to tell the small variations apart.

You will also need a list of the Sun, Moon, Planets, Nodes and Angles *from* your birth horoscope. There are many good places where you can get a horoscope. You can get a finely painted, hand-drawn horoscope from www.fishtailastrology.com but all you need for this project is your birth horoscope. The example horoscope, which belongs to Henry VIII, (Illustration *4) has the list of Sun, Moon, Planets, Nodes and Angels next to it so you can see exactly which information to take from a horoscope.

The next thing you need is an astrological ephemeris for the current year. You can buy a pamphlet for 1 year, a book for 50 years or you can find astrological ephemerides on-line. The following chapter explains how to understand an ephemeris.

Illustration *1

CONSTELLATIONS

ARIES

LEO

SAGITTARIUS

TAURUS

VIRGO

CAPRICORN

GEMINI

LIBRA

AQUARIUS

CANCER

SCORPIO

PISCES

Illustration *2

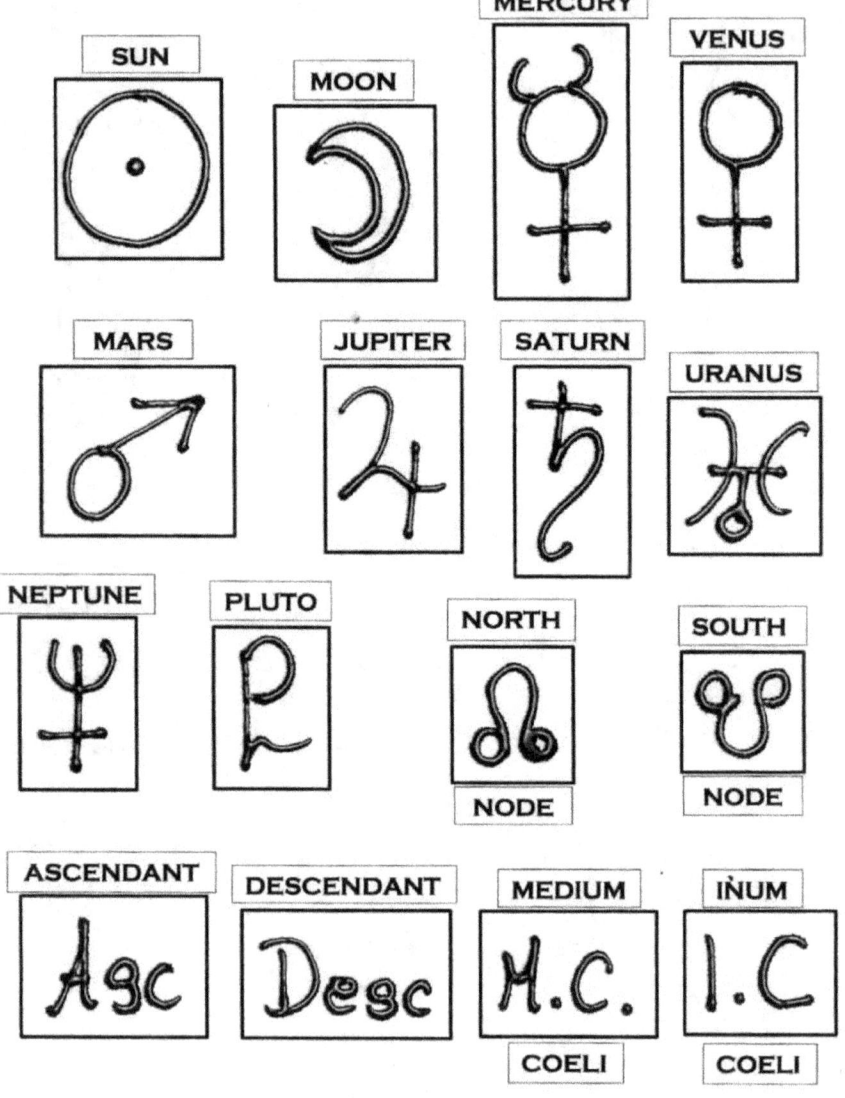

Illustration *3
SYMBOLS OF THE ASPECTS

ASPECTS

1 CONJUNCTION
2 TRINE
3 SQUARE
4 OPPOSITION
5 SEXTILE
6 BI-QUINTILE
7 QUINTILE
8 INCONJUNCT

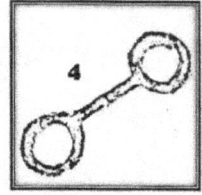

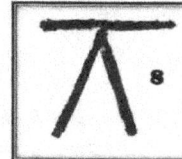

Illustration *4

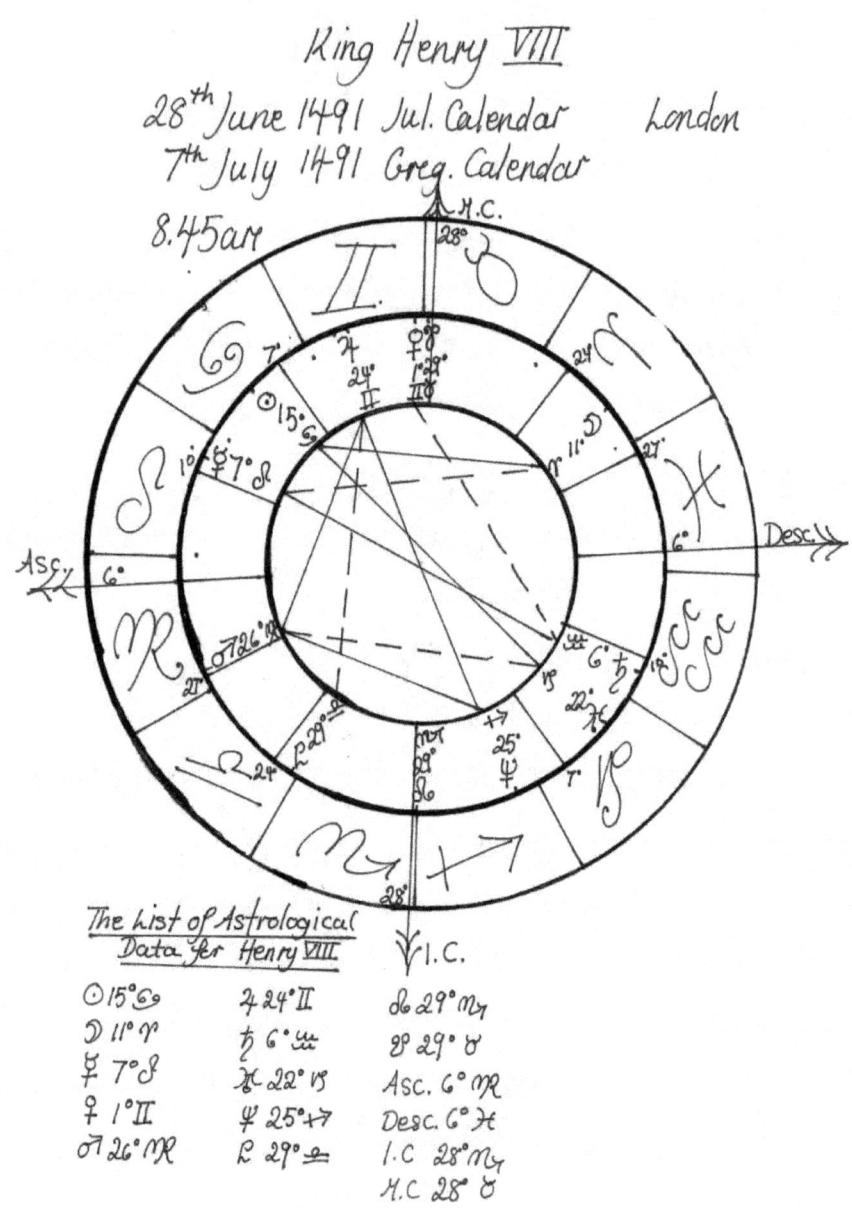

Understanding an Ephemeris

An ephemeris contains daily tables of the positions of the astrological bodies in the astrological constellations.

The symbols of the Planets are written on the top horizontal line of the ephemeris. Compare them with the symbols on illustration #2

The Planets, Sun, Moon and Nodes each move in different cycles. The tiny numbers in the ephemeris relate to the degree of the constellations they are in; each constellation has 30° (30° x 12 constellations = 360°) The M.C, I.C, Ascendant and Descendant are not in the ephemeris. This is because these are Angles. Angles are calculated to show the highest, lowest, east and west points of the ecliptic belt around the earth. The symbols of the constellations are on illustration #1

Some ephemerides have the motions of asteroids, midnight and noon Moon, Galactic Centre, phases of the Moon and latitudes but you do not need all of these to get started.

In the ephemeris the second column next to the date shows 3 sets of 2 numbers. This is the sidereal time for that day. Sidereal time is written in hours, minutes and seconds, as are the positions of astrological bodies in their constellations. Degrees, minutes and seconds are measured in multiples of 60. Sidereal time is also measured in multiples of 60 minutes and 24 hours, like ordinary clock time. The sidereal time is used for the calculation of a horoscope.[4] This project requires for a horoscope to be already drawn up so you do not need to worry about using sidereal time.

The third column shows the degree of the Sun in the constellation. The constellation is shown at the top of this column between the degrees and minutes. If the Sun is at 20° Sagittarius and natal Venus is at 22° Sagittarius, then the astrologer will wait two days to write in their journal under 'Sun Transit conjunct Venus Natal' (the Sun averages 1° a day). Although some Planets can be effective within orbs of a few degrees, when first learning how to follow your transits it is best to keep to the exact degree, in order that the correct subjective experience can be recognized.

In some ephemerides there is another column showing the declination of Sun which is useful

---

[4] There are courses for the budding astrologer to calculate horoscopes and transits as well as to understand how to work with astrology at Fishtail School of Mystical Arts.

for knowing how close in the sky Planets pass to the Sun.

The column after the Sun shows the Moon at noon, with the constellation it is in printed between the degrees and minutes. Notice how the Moon only spends about 2¼ days in each constellation.

Sometimes, between the Moon at noon and the Moon at midnight, there are other columns showing declination of the Moon, latitude and Node. To learn how to use astrology it is best to stay simple, for now. The Moon's position at midnight, depending on whether it comes before or after the Moon at noon, is the beginning of the new day. Most ephemerides have two columns for the Moon; one at noon and one at midnight. On average the Moon moves 13° in 24 hours.

After the Moon comes the column for the transiting North Node. Sometimes it is called the Mean position, sometimes the True position. The Nodes travel Retrograde most of the time. Next along is Mercury, which incidentally is often in Retrograde and considered the cause of awry communications. Then Venus, then Mars and usually Jupiter comes after Mars. However, some ephemerides put asteroids in here. After Jupiter there are Saturn, Uranus, Neptune and Pluto.

It is important to check the time zones for the ephemerides in order to calculate the Moon's correct position. Different ephemerides use different time zones and will affect the position given for the Moon. For example: an ephemeris which uses EST, will state 'Noon' but that 'Noon' will be at 5pm GMT. The Moon would have moved approximately 2½° in that time, which is significant. If using an ephemeris for a different time zone is unavoidable, then all that needs to be done is to convert to that time zone to find the Moon's position. I do not know of any ephemeris that would show sidereal time in any other time than GMT.

You will learn how to calculate the transits in the following pages. Astrologers look in the ephemeris for future dates too and after working with your transits you will soon discover what predictions are possible.

Extrapolating Correct Data from a Horoscope

Lay the ephemeris aside and look at your horoscope.

When you look at Illustration *4 you will see a list of astrological data underneath the horoscope. You will need to look at the symbol of the Astrological Body (in the middle ring) and at the symbols of the constellation (in the outer ring). Compare the symbols in Illustrations *1 & *2 to know the names of the symbols. The numbers, between the symbols, are the degrees that the astrological body is at in the given constellation.

Now if you look at the List of Astrological Data under Henry VIII's horoscope, then find the individual symbols within the middle circle, you will see that the symbols and degrees are the same.

With your own horoscope: look to the middle ring, carefully copy the symbols with their degrees. From the outer ring note the correct constellation for each symbol and make your own list.

The degree which the astrological body is at, in a given constellation, is what you will look for in the ephemeris. The ephemeris shows the degree astrological bodies are in a constellation at a given date.

Calculating Transits

You now have the list of astrological bodies from your birth horoscope and the ephemeris of the current year in front of you.

First Try Calculating Sun Transits

A transit of the Sun is when the Sun of the current year crosses the astrological bodies of your natal horoscope.

The easiest way is to start with the ephemeris of the current year, and look for your date of birth. In the 3rd column (the 1st is the date of the month, the 2nd is the sidereal time) look at the position of the Sun on your birthday. The position of the Sun is given in degrees, minutes and seconds. The constellation that the Sun is in is written between the degrees and minutes on the 1st of the month and the 21st of the month, when the Sun moves into the next sign.

Now check that the Sun in the ephemeris is at the same degree and constellation as your natal Sun. Your astrological birthday could be the day before or after your known birthday because of the difference between sidereal time and solar time.

The day that the Sun is at the same degree of your natal Sun in your horoscope is the transit – Transiting Sun conjunct Natal Sun.[5]

If any other Planets, Angles or Nodes are conjunct your natal Sun, they will also be transited by the Sun on your birthday.

After recognizing the solar transit on your birthday, check to see if you have any other Planets, Nodes or Angles near the same degree as your natal Sun. They may be at a degree before or after your Natal Sun, which means transits may be a few days apart.

Now look to the rest of your Planets, Nodes and Angles in your natal horoscope. Using the ephemeris, match the days when the Sun will be in the same constellation and the same degree as each astrological body. These are the transits of the Sun within the year of the ephemeris.

The last few pages of this manual are for you to write the dates of the coming transits.

---

[5] There is a wonderful practice of calculating a horoscope for the coming year from the exact time the transiting Sun conjuncts the Natal Sun, in degrees, minutes and seconds. The birthday horoscope for the current year gives insight as to issues that would need to be addressed that year.

Calculate Moon Transits

Each month the Moon will transit all of your natal Planets, Nodes and Angles, one by one. For instance, if you have Mars in Aries, Venus in Virgo, Sun, Mercury, Jupiter, Saturn and Neptune in Libra, you will be avidly filling in the Moon transits during the two days the Moon is in Libra. The order that the Moon transits the astrological bodies is dependent on your chart.

Occasionally, the Moon conjuncts the same place twice in one month, the difference arising because the Moon's position is at the very start or very end of a given constellation. When this happens you can just write your insights onto that same page.

Look then to the column for the Moon, in the ephemeris for the current year. Is it a midnight or noon ephemeris? The ephemeris should have it written in the column of the Moon. If it does not, you will need to find it in the introduction pages or on the webpage. On average, the Moon moves 13° in 24 hours. For example: Moon moves 11°54'40" in one day and in another day it may move 13°11'09" Should you feel you need greater exactitude, just calculate the Moon's movement over the 24 or 12 hours (dependant on whether the ephemeris has midnight and noon positions), for the particular day you have in mind.

The Moon's average movement:

24 hours	13°
12 hours	6½°
6 hours	3¼°
3 hours	1½°
2 hours	1°
1 hour	½°

Example #1: **If the Moon shown at Midnight is**

13° 25' 31" Gemini and your natal North Node is 22° 50' Gemini, you would calculate the Moon's transit to 22°50' Gemini thus: 13° 25' 31"

In 12 hours (Noon) Moon will move +6° 30'

Adding these gives   19° 55' 31"

To find how much extra time you need after 12 hours:

Natal North Node 22° 50' minus 19° 55' 31"

Note: In order to 'borrow' from the previous number you have to think ahead when subtracting degrees, minutes and seconds as they are based on 60 and not 10. (60 seconds makes 1 minute, 60 minutes makes 1 hour and so on. By adding 1 second to 23 hours, 59 minutes and 59 seconds, you get 24 hours but 24 hours is represented as 0 hours, 0 minutes and 0 seconds so you count back up again.) So right from the start, add 60 seconds and minus 1 minute from the top row.

22° 49' 60"

-19° 55' 31"

29" Note: You can only go so far till you have to 'borrow' again and add 60 minutes from degree column. Thus:

21° 109' 60"

- 19°   55' 31"

2° 54' 29" This number is the remainder needed for the Moon to travel after 12 hours that day to the degree of Natal North Node. 2° 54' 29" is virtually 3°. The Moon takes 6 hours to move 3°. So the original 12 hours (as we started at midnight) plus the 'nearly' 6 hours means the Transiting Moon conjunct Natal North Node would be a little before 6pm that day. You then would keep an eye out from 5pm till 7pm that day for the effects of this transit. When you keep an eye out for an hour either side of the allotted time you might see cause and effect. The Planets inspire causes but it is not unusual to miss the cause and see only the effect. Astrology books give interpretations of both cause and effect.

Example #2: **The Moon at noon is 4° 55' 35" Capricorn and Natal Mars is at 1°05' Capricorn.**

4° 55' 35"

-1° 50'

3° 05' 35" is the distance in time, on the given day, the Moon travels before noon from Natal Mars at 1°50' Capricorn. Which means it is approximately 6am when the Transiting Moon conjuncts Natal Mars.

Example #3: **The Moon at noon is 10° 22' 31" Taurus and Natal Saturn is 16° 47' Taurus.**

This is easier because in 12 hours the Moon moves 6½° so on this day the Moon will get to about 16° 47' not much before midnight. You will be watching from about 11pm.

Example #4: **It is even easier when the Moon is 1° 20' 35" Cancer at noon and your Ascendant is 3° 15' Cancer. You need 2°; that takes about 4** hours. So you expect the transit at 4pm. You need to watch between 3pm and 5pm that day.

The Moon does not transit in isolation. Although there may not be any specific link all of the time, you will probably notice that when the same Moon transits to a natal Planet in a different month, it feels slightly different. This can be because the rest of your natal chart is more in tune with the other transits and you just feel safer. For this project, what matters is that you take note of the manifestations that occur at the time of your transits. Cosmic Journal is set out to record and order this meticulous work but you can now record this work in your own journal.

Remember to convert the Moon's transit time back from UT to your Local Time.

This concludes how to calculate Moon transits. You can prepare some for the month in advance and write them in the back of this manual.

Calculating Transiting Nodes and Planets

The Nodes and Planets do not move as fast as the Moon so, like the Sun, they will be on the degree of one of your Natal astrological bodies for a day or two. Like the Sun, you will watch for the effect of that transit during the whole day(s).

The larger Planets can stay longer on the same degree. For instance, Jupiter usually stays at the same degree for 5 days. It is a good idea to earmark the day before and the day after for monitoring the effect of transiting Jupiter on one of your Natal Planets, Angles or Nodes. Over time, you will start noticing the effects of the larger Planets, when they are within a few degrees of your natal Planet, Node or Angle. You will notice with the larger Planets, that a new attitude is usurping your mind. You might think circumstances make it justified so you do not notice that the Cosmos and your Mind are in cahoots.

Mars can sometimes stay 2 days on a given degree. Saturn can stay a month or a couple of weeks, and Saturn might go back and forth over a certain degree over months. Uranus, Neptune and Pluto are similar and also take longer going back and forth. These remote Planets cause such significant changes within your psyche that you will be pleased, as you go through one of their transformations, to see that there is some reason behind it. For instance, a Neptune transit tends to cause lack of focus, a search for divine inspiration, as well as obsessive longings and fascinations for others. There is also a thirst for music (as well as other things along this line, including inebriation and escapism) in a person who could have been alienated to this mind-set previously. Big changes are likely with the bigger Planets. In the case of a Neptune transit you might join a commune, become a better musician or artist, become a martyr or even a victim, or begin a yoga practice.

During a Pluto transit over Venus a person could develop a more intense, passionate or jealous, possessive mind-set within a relationship. You learn to trust your doubts. Over-all, Pluto will not let you carry on dragging an old cloak about on your shoulders. These transits can go on for years; chipping away at the crusty parts of an outmoded part of your character, which had become like a shell, hiding the real, new emerging part of you.

The life-changing larger Planets can be triggered by smaller transits to the same Natal Planet. This is often a way of glimpsing how the transit will be moving through your psyche.

With astrology you come to understand the new parts of you that are growing. You are growing and becoming your better self all through your life. All through your life you are constantly adjusting to life, the meaning within you and the experiences around you. Astrology is an excellent map for this journey

Knowing What to Look For

When the time of the transit comes you need to know what to look for. Knowing what to look for will help you to attune to the energies of the Planetary influences. When I spent years inadvertently proving the accuracy of astrology, there were times when I would deliberately not know which transits were happening. Then, looking back over my journal, I sifted the events into their synchronized causes, pinpointing the key influences.

For this project you will need to have an idea of what you are looking for. You will need to know what the expression of each Planet is. Though you can follow your transits 'blind' and not know what to expect at all. This may take longer to recognize thoughts, feelings, inspirations and ideas but ultimately will also add to the validity of astrology.

If you do know the expressions of the Planets, be aware of the positive and negative manifestations of the same key-influence. How the key-influence manifests in your life is an indicator of your own inner wisdom. If the manifestation is negative, or not as positive as it could be, then this is your personal inner-growth signpost.

Having preconceived ideas makes it easier to find the inner field of action which relates to a specific transit. You might think that you are tricking yourself if you are looking for it, the point is, don't trick yourself. Be open; be real, even though it may take a few months to recognize inspirations and instigations.

It is enough to be aware of unconscious processes just after they have happened. You may be aware that you are acting kind of 'funny' in the throes of unconscious behaviour. The unconscious has a particular feel to it: to me it is like a fuzzy twilight and I am centred deep inside of myself, aware of actions but not why I am doing them. Not all unconscious behaviour is bad either; there will undoubtedly be some behaviour you really are quite pleased with. The next time you do behave 'unconsciously' you won't be so unconscious. You become more and more aware of parts of you and you can then change or accept them.

It seems to me there is a never ending field of unconsciousness in every second. Like the roots of a tree. Like the currents in the oceans. The field of unconscious activity will probably be the main field of your study. You will become conscious of what was once unconscious. Where do you look? Inside your own mind, your own thoughts and feelings become clearer and clearer.

Be aware that transits over Planets are different the opposite way round. For instance, a transit of Moon over Sun is different to Sun over Moon. Generally, the first will reveal a habit or need which requires integrating into consciousness; accepting and living with a part of you that had previously been unacknowledged. The latter will bring awareness of a need or habit. Similarly, Saturn transiting Mars is different to Mars transiting Saturn. In the first scenario Saturn will limit or hone successful action and in the second scenario Mars will invigorate you to take charge and do something.

Now you know when, where and what to look for, you will sail wide awake through your inner world. Your inner world is there whether you are aware of it or not. Isn't it better to be aware? Do not get caught up in judging yourself – just change what you need to. Remember you are a scientist, watching and recording impressions. This is magnificent work.

Knowing What to Write

Write about your feelings, your thoughts, inspirations, realizations, ideas. Write about people, or animals, you communicate with or meet or people you try to connect with. Write about your successes and failures for that day. Write about what you enjoyed or didn't enjoy. Only you know what is going on deep in the furnaces of your soul. Write for your ears.

Whilst it is important to notice manifestations of the keywords and known expressions of the Planets and astrological bodies involved in the transits, it is also important not to ignore what else is happening. This project is a true study; you will not need to pretend or exaggerate or fit anything in.

After a few months you will have a lot of recordings for Moon transits and some inner Planets. Cosmic Journal has a Facebook page or visit www.fishtailastrology.com/cosmic-journal to share your findings and read about what other people are discovering.

Preparing for Transits

The following pages are to prepare transits for the future. This practice helps prepare your mind for a way through changes ahead. For instance, if Uranus will transit your Moon and soon after Jupiter crosses your I.C and Saturn comes up to conjuncting your Mercury, you could meld their concepts together and see a process of finding a place to live that includes space for reflection and fun. If you do not consider the later transits, of Jupiter and Saturn, the Uranus transit conjunct Moon could force you to move suddenly with unnecessary upheaval and no plan. Your values change. So under Uranus transit Moon you may feel you need change and excitement but with no forethought you could find yourself mentally frustrated and unsettled later. This is just an example; there are other, similar, ways to interpret such a set of transits. The more you use your imagination the more possibilities will open up.

Astrologers use the time before a transit to till the soil and sow the seeds. Then when the time of the transit occurs, they reap the harvest. Astrologers work with clients leading them to deep, inner work. The client becomes more involved and aware of the part of their psyche they are working on. As individual astrologers you will work with a Planet of your choice, by exploring that Planet's nature within you. Imagination is the key which will open door after door. Your birth chart is the map which will save you going down one rabbit hole after another. Use your birth chart to keep returning to the umbrella meaning of the Planet.

Sometimes you will get a dream image of an archetype which expresses the astrological concept you had been working on. If you like it you can imagine living it. If you do not like it then unpick it more, from the fabric of your mind.

Astrological work is wonderful work. Your horoscope is your best counsellor. It reflects back every issue you raise and asks how you want it to be. Astrology is used to transmute our inner world to create the life attuned to us. We can trust our horoscope to not lead us astray, as we learn to trust ourselves to be the best we can be.

DATE	TRANSIT

DATE	TRANSIT

DATE	TRANSIT

DATE	TRANSIT

DATE	TRANSIT

NOTES: **notes about notes: new concepts, new ideas to check out later: draw the symbols and make them my own: the symbol which fascinates me most right now is....fascinations change as I develop: notes about other people who bring out a Planetary energy in me: notes:**

Also published by Fishtail Arts & Astrology:

Manual of Astrological Calculations 2019

Astro Journal 2018

Cosmic Journal 2018

Age of the Fishtail 2013

www.fishtailastrology.com

FB Fishtail Arts & Astrology

Just Cosmic by Rikki Blythe

Published by Fishtail Arts & Astrology

 2018

www.ingramcontent.com/pod-product-compliance
Lightning Source LLC
Chambersburg PA
CBHW071323080526
44587CB00018B/3329